Play It Smart

Playground Safety

How to Be Safe!

by Jill Urban Donahue   illustrated by Bob Masheris

Special thanks to our advisers for their expertise:
Sandi Schnorenberg, Associate Deputy Director
Mankato (Minnesota) Public Safety

Terry Flaherty, Ph.D., Professor of English
Minnesota State University, Mankato

PICTURE WINDOW BOOKS
Minneapolis, Minnesota

Editor: Jill Kalz
Designer: Abbey Fitzgerald
Page Production: Melissa Kes
Art Director: Nathan Gassman
Associate Managing Editor: Christianne Jones
The illustrations in this book were created digitally.

Picture Window Books
151 Good Counsel Drive
P.O. Box 669
Mankato, MN 56002-0669
877-845-8392
www.picturewindowbooks.com

Printed in the United States of America.

 All books published by Picture Window Books
are manufactured with paper containing at least
10 percent post-consumer waste.

Library of Congress Cataloging-in-Publication Data
Donahue, Jill L. (Jill Lynn), 1967-
Play it smart : playground safety / by Jill Urban Donahue ;
illustrated by Bob Masheris.
p. cm. — (How to be safe!)
Includes index.
ISBN-13: 978-1-4048-4823-8 (library binding)
1. Playgrounds—Safety measures—Juvenile literature.
I. Masheris, Robert, ill. II. Title.
GV424.D66 2008
796.06'8—dc22   2008006433

Playgrounds are great places to play with your friends. But if you are not careful, you could get hurt. If you follow playground safety rules, you will have a fun time on all kinds of playgrounds!

Becca, Mia, and Andy ask their parents if they can go to the playground. They listen to their parents explain the rules.

Becca, Mia, and Andy want to play safe.

Safety Tip

Don't go to a playground alone. If an adult you know can't go with you, take along at least one friend.

5

It's a sunny day. Becca helps Andy and Mia put on sunscreen. She makes sure they put on closed-toed shoes, too.

Safety Tip

Don't wear clothes with drawstrings to the playground. The strings can get caught in playground equipment.

At the playground, Becca puts her backpack
by the fence. She keeps it out of the play area.
She doesn't want anyone to trip over it.

Safety Tip

It's best to leave your backpack, jacket, and other things at home. If you have to bring things to the playground, keep them where you can see them. But keep them out of the play area.

Becca, Mia, and Andy play catch. Andy drops the ball. It rolls into the street. Andy waits for the ball to stop rolling. He looks for cars before scooping up the ball.

Safety Tip

Don't run into the street after a ball or toy. Drivers might not see you.

11

An ice-cream truck drives past the playground. Mia wants to follow it. Becca tells Mia they need to stay together.

Safety Tip

Never walk away from the playground by yourself. And never go anywhere with a stranger.

The climbing wall is still wet from last night's rain. Becca decides not to play on it. Wet surfaces can be very slippery.

Safety Tip

Before playing, check the ground around the play area. Make sure there are no sharp objects that you could step on.

Andy carefully climbs the steps to the top of the slide. He takes one step at a time. He holds onto the handrails.

Safety Tip

Never try to walk up a slide. You may slip. Or someone might come down and knock you over.

Mia waits her turn at the bottom of the steps.

Becca, Mia, and Andy take turns going down the slide. They go feet first. They move away from the bottom of the slide as soon as they land.

Safety Tip
If you or a friend gets hurt while playing, tell an adult right away.

Andy and Mia sit on the swings. They hold on with both hands while Becca pushes them.

Safety Tip
Never walk in front of moving swings.

Becca, Mia, and Andy are careful on the playground. They stay together and pay attention to things going on around them.

Becca, Mia, and Andy play safe and have fun!

To Learn More

More Books to Read

Cuyler, Margery. *Please Play Safe! Penguin's Guide to Playground Safety.* New York: Scholastic Press, 2006.

Pancella, Peggy. *Playground Safety.* Chicago: Heinemann Library, 2005.

Raatma, Lucia. *Safety on the Playground and Outdoors.* Chanhassen, Minn.: Child's World, 2005.

Thomas, Pat. *I Can Be Safe: A First Look at Safety.* Hauppauge, N.Y.: Barron's Educational Series, 2003.

On the Web

FactHound offers a safe, fun way to find Web sites related to topics in this book. All of the sites on FactHound have been researched by our staff.

1. Visit *www.facthound.com*
2. Type in this special code: 1404848231
3. Click on the FETCH IT button.

Your trusty FactHound will fetch the best sites for you!

Index

Look for all of the books in the How to Be Safe! series:

Contain the Flame: Outdoor Fire Safety

Play It Safe: Playground Safety

Ride Right: Bicycle Safety

Say No and Go: Stranger Safety